Financial Infidelity

Stop Lying to Him, Stop Lying to Yourself, and Fix Your Relationship with Money Before It Costs You Everything

By **Essence Coffey**

Fire & Inspire Publishing LLC

COPYRIGHT PAGE

Published by:

Fire & Inspire Publishing LLC

ISBN: 979-8-90083-502-0

This book is intended for educational and informational purposes only. It is not a substitute for financial, legal, or psychological advice. The author assumes no responsibility for any outcomes resulting from the use of this material.

All scenarios are based on common behavioral patterns and are intended for educational and reflective purposes.

SERIES PAGE

The Relationship Truth Series™ by Essence Coffey

Books that say what people feel—but don't say aloud.

- Emotional Boundaries: Why Oversharing Is a Form of Self-Betrayal
- What the Hell Is a Work Wife?
- Financial Infidelity *(You are here)*
- The Woman He Wasted No Time Replacing™
- When a Woman Stays, When a Woman Goes™

Each book is designed to confront, clarify, and correct the patterns that quietly destroy relationships.

PUBLISHER PAGE

Fire & Inspire Publishing LLC

Building bold voices.
Publishing truth that disrupts denial.
Creating books that don't just inspire—but change behavior.

DEDICATION

To the woman who knows something isn't right...
but hasn't said it aloud yet.

And to the one who is ready to stop explaining, stop hiding,
and finally get honest—with herself first.

About Essence Coffey

Essence Coffey is known for saying what most people avoid.

Her work blends emotional intelligence, real-life patterns, and unfiltered truth to help women confront the behaviors that keep them stuck—especially in relationships, identity, and self-worth.

She doesn't write to soothe denial.
She writes to expose it.

Her books are for women who are ready to stop pretending, start seeing clearly, and move differently.

TRIGGER NOTE

This book contains direct and honest conversations about financial behavior, secrecy, and relationship dynamics.

Some sections may feel uncomfortable.
That discomfort is intentional.

Not to shame you—but to help you see clearly.

Read with honesty. Reflect with courage. Apply with discipline.

HOW TO READ THIS BOOK

This is not a passive read.

This is not a “that’s interesting” kind of book.

This is a **sit with it, reflect on it, and act on it** type of book.

As you read:

- Pause when something hits
- Be honest instead of defensive
- Don’t skip the uncomfortable parts
- Use the reflection sections

Because the goal is not to finish this book.

The goal is to **change what needs to be changed.**

AUTHOR'S NOTE

Let's be clear from the beginning.

This is not about blaming men.
This is not about controlling women.
And this is not about making you feel small.

This is about telling the truth.

Because financial infidelity doesn't start with money.

It starts with:

Avoidance.
Emotional decision-making.
And the quiet belief that "it's not that serious."

Until it is.

You can be a good woman and still mishandle money.
You can love someone and still break trust.
You can mean well and still create damage.

This book is not here to shame you.

It's here to interrupt the pattern—before it costs you something you care about.

PREFACE

He loves you.

He really does.

He's patient.
He's trying.
He's showing up.

And you?

You love him too.

But somewhere between "I deserve this" and "it's not that much"...
you started hiding things.

Insignificant things at first.

Then patterns.

Then behavior.

And now?

You're managing what he sees... instead of telling the truth.

That's not just spending.

That's secrecy.

And secrecy in any form?

Breaks trust.

This book is not here to accuse you.

It’s here to wake you up.

Because the same way you expect honesty, stability, and respect in love…

You must bring that same energy to money.

INTRODUCTION

Let's not pretend.

You didn't pick this book randomly.

Something you already know:

- Your spending isn't as controlled as you say
- Your honesty hasn't been as consistent as it should be
- Your habits aren't aligning with the life you say you want

And instead of addressing it directly…

You've been:

- Minimizing it
- Justifying it
- Avoiding it

But here's the truth:

Financial infidelity doesn't always look dramatic.

It looks like:

- "I'm not going to mention this one"

- “I’ll fix it before he notices”
- “It’s really not that serious”

Until one day…

It is.

This book is going to:

✓ Call out the behavior

✓ Break down why it’s happening

✓ Show you how it damages trust

✓ Give you a real path to change

Because this isn’t about money.

It’s about honesty.

And once that’s off?

Everything else follows.

Chapter 1 — This Is Not "Just Spending": Defining Financial Infidelity

Language shapes perception, and perception determines whether behavior is corrected or continued. For this reason, the tendency to label problematic financial behavior as "just spending" is not only inaccurate—it is dangerous. It allows individuals to engage in patterns of concealment while maintaining the illusion that nothing serious is occurring. However, when examined closely, the issue extends far beyond the act of purchasing. It is not the transaction itself that defines the problem, but the intentional separation between what is done and what is disclosed.

Financial infidelity is best understood as a breach of relational transparency. It occurs when one partner knowingly engages in financial behavior that is inconsistent with the expectations of the relationship and chooses to conceal or distort that behavior rather than communicate it openly. This concealment does not require large sums of money or dramatic actions. In many cases, it develops through small, repeated decisions that appear insignificant in isolation but collectively form a pattern of dishonesty.

What distinguishes financial infidelity from poor monetary management is awareness. Individuals engaged in this behavior often recognize, at some level, that their actions would require explanation if brought to light. This recognition is evidenced by the hesitation that precedes disclosure, the internal dialogue that justifies the decision, and the subsequent effort to manage what is seen versus what is hidden. These elements indicate that the behavior is not accidental. It is intentional, even if that intention is minimized or reframed.

The challenge, therefore, lies in accurately naming the behavior. As long as it is softened through language—described as "treating oneself" or "not that serious"—it remains insulated from accountability. By defining it as financial infidelity, the behavior is placed within its appropriate context: not as a personal habit, but as a relational issue that directly impacts trust, stability, and mutual understanding.

Chapter 2 — The Internal Narrative: How Self-Justification Sustains the Pattern

Behavior rarely exists without justification. In the case of financial infidelity, this justification often takes the form of internal narratives that reduce discomfort while preserving the behavior itself. These narratives are not random; they are structured, repeated, and refined over time. They allow individuals to engage in actions that conflict with their stated values while maintaining a sense of coherence in their self-image.

Common forms of justification include statements such as "it is just this one time," "it is not that serious," or "it can be fixed later." Each of these statements serves a specific psychological function. They minimize the perceived impact of the behavior, delay accountability, and create a temporary sense of control. However, they do not eliminate the underlying issue. Instead, they allow it to persist without direct confrontation.

What is particularly significant about these narratives is that they often emerge before the behavior has fully developed into a pattern. In other words, the justification precedes the escalation. By reframing the initial instances of concealment as manageable or insignificant, individuals create the conditions under which the behavior can expand. Over time, the narratives evolve to accommodate increasingly complex patterns, including the management of multiple transactions, accounts, or explanations.

This process highlights the importance of examining not only what is done, but how it is explained internally. The language individuals use with themselves reveals the degree of awareness present in their behavior. If an action requires justification, it is unlikely to be neutral. The presence of explanation indicates the presence of conflict, and conflict is often the first indicator that behavior is misaligned with values.

Chapter 3 — Everyday Expressions of Financial Infidelity

To fully understand financial infidelity, it must be observed in its everyday form. It does not exist solely in extreme scenarios, such as undisclosed debt or hidden accounts of significant value. Instead, it is embedded within routine actions that have been normalized through repetition.

One common expression involves the intentional omission of information. An individual may make a purchase that exceeds agreed limits or falls outside shared expectations and choose not to disclose it. When questioned, the response may be vague or minimized, reducing the perceived significance of the transaction. This behavior is often justified as a means of avoiding unnecessary conflict, but it reflects a decision to prioritize personal comfort over relational transparency.

Another form involves the use of hidden financial channels. This may include undisclosed accounts, credit lines, or payment platforms that operate outside the awareness of one's partner. While these tools may be framed as expressions of independence, their concealment raises important questions about intention. If the behavior is truly harmless, there would be no need to hide it.

A third expression is the cyclical pattern of overspending followed by temporary corrective action. In this scenario, the individual recognizes that they have exceeded reasonable limits and attempts to compensate through short-term adjustments, such as shifting funds or delaying payments. However, these adjustments do not address the underlying behavior. Instead, they allow the cycle to continue, reinforcing the pattern over time.

Finally, emotional spending represents a particularly pervasive form of financial infidelity. In this context, purchases are made in response to emotional states rather than practical needs. While this behavior may appear personal, it becomes relational when it is concealed or misrepresented. The individual is not only managing their emotions through spending but also managing the perception of that spending within the relationship.

Chapter 4 — Confronting Recognition: The Moment of Discomfort

Recognition is often accompanied by discomfort, and this discomfort serves a critical function. It signals that the individual is encountering a discrepancy between their behavior and their values. However, rather than engaging with this discomfort directly, many individuals respond by attempting to neutralize it through comparison, justification, or deflection.

This process may involve minimizing the behavior by comparing it to more extreme scenarios or redirecting attention to perceived shortcomings in the partner. While these strategies may reduce immediate discomfort, they do not resolve the underlying issue. Instead, they delay the moment of accountability, allowing the pattern to persist.

The challenge at this stage is to resist the impulse to explain or defend. Explanation, when used prematurely, often serves as a barrier to recognition rather than a pathway to understanding. True recognition requires a willingness to observe behavior without modification, to acknowledge patterns without immediately reframing them, and to accept the implications of those patterns without attempting to soften their impact.

This moment is pivotal because it represents a shift from passive awareness to active acknowledgment. Once behavior is recognized clearly, it cannot be easily dismissed. The individual is faced with a choice: to continue the pattern with full awareness or to begin the process of change.

Chapter 5 — The Broader Impact: Why This Behavior Matters

It is a common misconception that financial behavior exists in isolation. Financial infidelity has far-reaching implications that extend beyond the immediate transaction. At its core, it affects trust—the foundational element of any stable relationship.

Trust is built through consistency between words and actions. When an individual presents one version of their behavior while engaging in another, this consistency is disrupted. Even if the discrepancy is not immediately identified, it creates subtle shifts in relational dynamics. These shifts may manifest as increased questioning, reduced confidence, or a general sense of uncertainty.

Over time, these subtle changes accumulate. The relationship may not experience a single moment of rupture, but rather a gradual erosion of stability. The partner may begin to rely less on verbal assurances and more on observation, seeking to verify rather than assume. This shift, while often unspoken, represents a meaningful change in the relational environment.

Equally important is the internal impact on the individual engaging in the behavior. Maintaining a pattern of concealment requires cognitive effort and emotional management. It creates a division between what is known internally and what is presented externally, which can lead to feelings of anxiety, inconsistency, and diminished self-trust.

For these reasons, financial infidelity must be understood as more than a financial issue. It is a behavioral pattern with relational and psychological consequences. Addressing it requires not only changes in spending, but changes in communication, transparency, and self-perception.

Chapter 6 — Naming the Behavior as the First Act of Change

Change cannot occur in the absence of clarity. As long as behavior is described in vague or softened terms, it remains resistant to intervention. Naming the behavior accurately is therefore not an act of judgment, but an act of precision.

By identifying the pattern as financial infidelity, the individual removes the ambiguity that allows it to persist. This naming process does not assign moral failure; it establishes factual understanding. It acknowledges that the behavior involves intentional concealment, that it affects relational trust, and that it requires deliberate change.

Once the behavior is named, it becomes visible in a new way. Actions that were previously dismissed as minor or isolated are recognized as components of a larger pattern. This recognition disrupts normalization, making it more difficult to continue the behavior without conscious awareness.

At this point, the individual is no longer operating within uncertainty. The pattern has been identified, its implications have been understood, and its presence has been acknowledged. This creates a moment of decision. The individual must determine whether to maintain the existing pattern or to initiate change.

This decision marks the transition from recognition to responsibility. It is not defined by immediate perfection, but by a willingness to engage with the behavior honestly and consistently. Without this willingness, no amount of strategy or planning will produce meaningful results.

End of Part I Reflection

Reflection at this stage requires a deliberate and structured approach. It is necessary to move beyond general acknowledgment and into specific identification of behavior. This involves examining not only what actions have been taken, but how frequently they occur, under what conditions they arise, and what outcomes they produce.

Equally important is the examination of internal language. The phrases used to justify or minimize behavior provide valuable insight into the mechanisms that sustain it. Identifying these phrases allows individuals to recognize when they are engaging in self-protection rather than self-assessment.

Finally, reflection must include an honest evaluation of patterns. Is the behavior isolated, or does it repeat across different contexts? Does it occur under specific emotional conditions, or does it appear regardless of circumstance? These questions are not intended to assign blame, but to establish clarity.

Clarity, in this context, is not optional. It is the foundation upon which all meaningful change is built. Once behavior is seen accurately, it can no longer be dismissed as accidental or insignificant. It becomes a defined pattern, and defined patterns can be addressed with intention.

PART II — THE BEHAVIOR BREAKDOWN

At this stage, it is no longer sufficient to acknowledge that a problem exists. Recognition without specificity allows behavior to remain abstract, and abstract problems are rarely corrected. What must occur now is a transition from general awareness to precise observation. This requires removing emotional cushioning, eliminating interpretive language, and examining behavior as it presents—not as it is intended, not as it is justified, and not as it is remembered after the fact.

Behavior, when observed accurately, is often far more structured than individuals are willing to admit. What is spontaneous or situational is frequently patterned, repeated, and reinforced through familiarity. These patterns are not random occurrences; they are systems. They involve triggers, predictable responses, and outcomes that, while temporarily relieving, sustain the cycle. Understanding this structure is critical, because one cannot interrupt a system that has not been clearly identified.

The goal of this section is not to analyze motivation—that will come later—but to isolate the behaviors themselves. This distinction is important. Many individuals attempt to explain their actions before they have fully examined them. This leads to rationalization rather than change. By focusing strictly on observable actions, the conversation becomes grounded rather than interpretation.

Chapter 6 — The Package, the Receipt, and the Pre-Prepared Lie

One of the most revealing indicators of financial infidelity is not the purchase itself, but the preparation that accompanies it. The moment an item is acquired, attention shifts from the object to the narrative that will surround it. This shift is immediate and often automatic. Before the package is even opened, the individual is already considering how the transaction will be framed, whether it will be disclosed, and how it will be explained if questioned.

This anticipatory behavior is significant because it demonstrates awareness. The need to prepare a response indicates that the action is not neutral. If the purchase were fully aligned with shared expectations, there would be no need for narrative management. The existence of this preparation reveals an internal recognition that the behavior may not withstand direct scrutiny.

In practical terms, this often manifests as a sequence of small but deliberate actions. The package may be retrieved quickly to avoid attention. Receipts are discarded immediately, not out of convenience, but to eliminate evidence. Tags are removed before the item is introduced into the shared environment, reducing the likelihood of inquiry. These actions, while individually minor, collectively form a system of concealment.

What is particularly important to note is that this system operates independently of external pressure. In many cases, the partner has not yet asked a question, made an accusation, or expressed concern. The concealment occurs preemptively. This indicates that the behavior is not reactive, it is initiative-taking. It is not driven by confrontation, but by the anticipation of it.

The repetition of this process reinforces the behavior. Each successful instance of concealment reduces internal resistance, making future instances easier and more automatic. Over time, what began as a conscious effort becomes habitual. The individual is no longer making isolated decisions; they are operating within an established pattern.

Chapter 7 — Buy Now, Pay Later: Deferred Accountability

The introduction of delayed payment systems adds another layer of complexity to financial behavior. While these systems are often marketed as tools for convenience, their psychological impact extends far beyond financial flexibility. They create a temporal separation between decision and consequence, allowing individuals to engage in behavior without immediately confronting its full implications.

In the context of financial infidelity, this separation becomes particularly problematic. The decision to purchase is made in the present, but the accountability associated with that decision is distributed across the future. This fragmentation allows individuals to rationalize behavior that might otherwise be avoided if the full cost were immediately visible.

The internal dialogue that accompanies these decisions often reflects this distortion. Statements such as "I will manage it later" or "It is not due right now" function as mechanisms of delay. They shift focus away from the present action and toward an imagined future resolution. However, this future resolution is rarely addressed with the same urgency as the initial decision. Instead, it becomes another element within the broader pattern of avoidance.

What is often overlooked is that this behavior does not merely postpone monetary responsibility; it postpones relational transparency. Each delayed payment represents a future moment in which explanation may be required. The narrative becomes more complex as more moments build up.

This creates a layered form of concealment. The person is actively overseeing present conduct while also forecasting and preparing for forthcoming disclosures. This continuous management requires cognitive effort, reinforcing the pattern and making disengagement increasingly difficult.

Chapter 8 — Emotional Spending as Behavioral Conditioning

Emotional spending is frequently misunderstood as a matter of poor impulse control. While impulse plays a role, this interpretation is incomplete. Emotional spending is more accurately understood as a conditioned response—a learned behavior that associates financial transactions with emotional regulation.

When an individual experiences discomfort, whether in the form of stress, frustration, boredom, or emotional depletion, the desire for relief becomes immediate. Spending provides a rapid and accessible means of altering emotional state. The act of selecting, purchasing, and acquiring an item introduces a sense of control, novelty, and temporary satisfaction. This creates a reinforcing loop.

Over time, the brain begins to associate spending with relief. The behavior becomes less about the item itself and more about the emotional shift it produces. This is why individuals often struggle to recall what they purchased, even when they clearly remember how they felt before and after the transaction. The purchase is not the objective; the emotional transition is.

This conditioning process is strengthened through repetition. Each time spending successfully alters emotional state, the association is reinforced. Eventually, the behavior becomes automatic. The individual does not consciously decide to spend; they respond to emotion in the only way they have trained themselves to.

This distinction is critical because it reframes the issue. The problem is not a lack of discipline in isolation. It is the presence of an established coping mechanism. Addressing this behavior requires more than restriction; it requires interruption and replacement.

Chapter 9 — Financial Avoidance and the Illusion of Protection

Avoidance is often misinterpreted as inaction. It is an active behavior—one that involves deliberate disengagement from information that may produce discomfort. In the context of financial patterns, avoidance typically manifests as a refusal to review accounts, monitor spending, or engage with financial data.

This behavior is frequently justified as a form of self-preservation. Individuals may argue that they are "protecting their peace" by not engaging with stressful information. However, this interpretation is misleading. Avoidance does not eliminate the underlying issue; it merely postpones awareness of it.

The psychological mechanism at play here is straightforward. By not observing the consequences of their actions, individuals reduce immediate discomfort. However, this reduction is temporary. The underlying reality remains unchanged, and in many cases, continues to deteriorate.

This creates a cycle in which avoidance leads to increased instability, which in turn increases the desire to avoid. The individual becomes trapped in a feedback loop that reinforces both the behavior and its consequences.

What makes this pattern particularly resistant to change is that it provides immediate relief. Unlike initiative-taking behaviors, which often require effort and produce delayed benefits, avoidance offers instant emotional comfort. This immediate reward makes it difficult to disrupt, even when the long-term consequences are clearly understood.

Chapter 10 — The Normalization of Minimization

Minimization functions as the cognitive framework that supports all other behaviors within this pattern. It allows individuals to reinterpret their actions in ways that reduce perceived severity, thereby preserving self-image and avoiding the need for change.

This process is subtle and often unconscious. It involves the consistent downscaling of behavior—reducing frequency, impact, or significance through comparative reasoning. Statements such as "It is not that much," "It is not that often," or "It could be worse" serve as tools for maintaining the status quo.

The effectiveness of minimization lies in its plausibility. These statements are not entirely false. The behavior may not be extreme, the frequency may not be constant, and the impact may not be catastrophic. However, this partial truth is used to obscure the larger pattern.

By focusing on individual instances rather than cumulative effect, minimization prevents accurate assessment. It shifts attention away from patterns and toward isolated events, making it difficult to recognize the behavior as a system.

Over time, this framework becomes self-reinforcing. Each instance of minimization reduces the likelihood of intervention, allowing the behavior to continue. As the pattern persists, the threshold for what is considered “serious” increases, further delaying recognition.

End of Part II Reflection

At this point, reflection must be approached with precision rather than generality. It is no longer sufficient to acknowledge that certain behaviors occur; the focus must shift toward identifying their frequency, context, and consistency. This requires examining not only what actions are repeated, but also the conditions under which they occur and the outcomes they produce.

Attention should be given to triggers. Behavioral patterns do not emerge without cause. Identifying the emotional, environmental, or situational factors that precede these actions provides critical insight into their function. Equally important is the recognition of avoidance—specifically, the areas in which engagement with reality has been intentionally limited.

Minimization must also be addressed directly. This involves challenging the narratives that have been used to reduce the perceived significance of behavior. Rather than comparing actions to more extreme scenarios, the focus should remain on accuracy.

What is occurring, how often it occurs, and what it creates over time.

The purpose of this reflection is not to induce guilt, but to establish clarity. Without clarity, behavior remains abstract and therefore resistant to change. With clarity, patterns become visible, and once visible, they can no longer be dismissed as accidental or misunderstood. This recognition marks the transition from passive awareness to active accountability.

PART III — THE PSYCHOLOGY BEHIND IT

At this stage, it becomes necessary to move beyond observation and into explanation. Behavior, once identified, must be understood within the context that produces it. Without this understanding, attempts at change often remain superficially focused on controlling actions rather than addressing the conditions that generate them. This distinction is critical. Behavior that appears irrational on the surface frequently reveals a coherent structure when examined at a deeper level.

Human behavior is rarely random. It is patterned, conditioned, and reinforced over time. What may initially appear as inconsistency or lack of discipline is often the result of learned responses to emotional, environmental, or cognitive triggers. These responses develop gradually, shaped by repetition and strengthened through reinforcement. As a result, individuals may find themselves engaging in behaviors that contradict their stated goals, not because they lack awareness, but because the underlying pattern has not been disrupted.

Understanding the psychological framework of financial infidelity requires acknowledging that the behavior serves a function. It provides relief, control, validation, or avoidance. Until that function is identified, the behavior will continue to reappear, even when consciously resisted. This is why individuals often experience cycles of temporary improvement followed by relapse. They attempt to eliminate the behavior without replacing the function it serves.

The purpose of this section is to examine these underlying mechanisms. Not to excuse the behavior, but to explain it. Because explanation, when grounded in accuracy, creates the possibility of interruption. Without it, change remains dependent on willpower alone, a resource that is inconsistent and easily depleted.

Chapter 11 — Emotional Response and the Spending Loop

At its core, emotional spending is not a financial issue, it is a regulatory one. It represents an attempt to alter internal states through external action. When individuals experience discomfort, whether mild or intense, the instinct to resolve that discomfort becomes immediate. This urgency often bypasses logical evaluation, prioritizing relief over consequence.

The act of spending introduces a rapid shift in emotional state. It provides stimulation, distraction, and a sense of control, all within a fleeting period. This shift is not incidental; it is reinforcing. Each time spending successfully reduces discomfort, the brain registers the behavior as effective. Over time, this creates an associative loop in which emotional discomfort automatically triggers the desire to spend.

This loop operates with increasing efficiency as it is repeated. The individual no longer engages in conscious decision-making at each stage. Instead, the process becomes automatic: discomfort arises, action follows, and temporary relief is achieved. The speed of this cycle reduces the opportunity for interruption, making the behavior appear impulsive when it is, in fact, conditioned.

What complicates this dynamic further is the temporary nature of the relief provided. The emotional shift achieved through spending is short-lived, often followed by secondary emotions such as guilt, anxiety, or regret. These secondary emotions may then trigger additional spending, reinforcing the loop. The individual is not merely engaging in a single behavior; they are sustaining a cycle that perpetuates itself.

Understanding this loop reframes the issue. The problem is not simply that spending occurs, but that it has become the default response to discomfort. Addressing this requires more than restriction. It requires the development of alternative responses that can fulfill the same regulatory function without creating additional consequences.

Chapter 12 — Control, Stability, and the Illusion of Agency

In environments where individuals feel a lack of control, they often seek areas in which control can be asserted. Financial decisions provide a readily accessible avenue for this assertion. The ability to choose, acquire, and possess creates a sense of agency, even when other aspects of life feel uncertain or unpredictable.

This dynamic is particularly relevant in the context of financial infidelity. When individuals experience instability, whether emotional, relational, or situational, it may turn to spending as a means of reestablishing control. The act of purchasing becomes symbolic. It represents the ability to decide, to create an outcome, and to influence one's environment.

However, this sense of control is illusory. While the immediate act of purchasing may create a feeling of agency, it often introduces additional instability in the long term. Financial strain, relational tension, and internal conflict may all increase because of the behavior. The individual is therefore engaging in a strategy that provides short-term control at the expense of long-term stability.

This contradiction is central to understanding the behavior. The individual is not seeking to create instability; they are attempting to resolve it. However, the method they are using is inherently unsustainable. It addresses the symptom of control—without addressing the source.

Recognizing this pattern requires a shift in perspective. Control must be redefined not as the ability to act in the moment, but as the ability to regulate behavior over time. True control is not demonstrated through immediate action, but through the capacity to pause, evaluate, and respond intentionally.

Chapter 13 — Identity, Image, and External Validation

Financial behavior is not only influenced by internal states, but also by external perceptions. Individuals often engage in spending patterns that align with the identity they wish to project, rather than the reality of their current circumstances. This alignment serves both a social and psychological function, reinforcing self-concept and influencing how one is perceived by others.

In this context, spending becomes a tool for identity construction. Purchases are selected not solely for their utility, but for their symbolic value. They communicate messages about success, stability, and self-worth. These messages may be directed outward, toward others, or inward, reinforcing the individual's perception of themselves.

The challenge arises when this constructed identity diverges significantly from financial reality. Maintaining the image requires continued spending, which may exceed available resources. This creates pressure, both financial and psychological, as the individual attempts to sustain a narrative that is not fully supported by their circumstances.

This dynamic is further complicated by the role of validation. Positive feedback, whether explicit or implied, reinforces the behavior. Compliments, recognition, or even internal satisfaction strengthen the association between spending and self-worth. Over time, this association becomes embedded, making it difficult to separate identity from financial behavior.

Addressing this pattern requires a reevaluation of the relationship between identity and action. It involves distinguishing between who one is and what one displays. Without this distinction, spending will continue to serve as a mechanism for validation, rather than a tool for practical decision-making.

Chapter 14 — Entitlement Framing and Boundary Erosion

The belief that one “deserves” certain outcomes can function as both a motivator and a rationalization. In the context of financial behavior, this belief often shifts from a legitimate acknowledgment of effort to a justification for bypassing limits. The phrase “I deserve this” becomes a conclusion rather than a consideration, ending the decision-making process prematurely.

This shift is subtle but significant. It transforms a reflective statement into a directive, reducing the likelihood of critical evaluation. The individual no longer asks whether the purchase is appropriate or sustainable; they assert that it is justified based on effort or circumstance.

While it is true that individuals deserve rest, reward, and enjoyment, these outcomes must be balanced with responsibility. When entitlement is used to override boundaries, it undermines the very stability those boundaries are intended to create. The result is a pattern in which immediate gratification is prioritized over long-term consistency.

This pattern is particularly resistant to change because it is framed positively. Unlike behaviors that are clearly recognized as problematic, entitlement-based decisions are often perceived as self-affirming. This perception reduces internal resistance, allowing the behavior to continue with minimal challenge.

To address this dynamic, the concept of deserving must be reframed. Rather than serving as a justification for action, it should function as one factor among many in the decision-making process. Effort and responsibility must be considered together, ensuring that reward does not come at the expense of stability.

Chapter 15 — Avoidance, Shame, and the Maintenance of the Cycle

Avoidance and shame are linked within this behavioral pattern. When individuals become aware of discrepancies between their actions and their values, they may experience discomfort that is difficult to process. Rather than addressing this discomfort directly, they may engage in avoidance, limiting exposure to information that would reinforce it.

This avoidance can take many forms, including delaying financial review, minimizing conversations, or reframing behavior to reduce its perceived impact. While these strategies provide temporary relief, they do not resolve the underlying issue. Instead, they contribute to the maintenance of the cycle by preventing full recognition of the problem.

Shame plays a critical role in this process. Unlike guilt, which is focused on specific actions, shame is often associated with self-perception. It involves a sense of inadequacy or failure that extends beyond behavior. This broader emotional response can make direct engagement with the issue more difficult, as it feels personally threatening rather than situational.

The interaction between avoidance and shame creates a self-sustaining loop. Behavior leads to awareness, awareness leads to discomfort, and discomfort leads to avoidance. This avoidance prevents resolution, allowing the behavior to continue and the cycle to repeat.

Breaking this cycle requires a shift in approach. Rather than attempting to eliminate discomfort, individuals must learn to tolerate it long enough to engage with the underlying issue. This involves separating behavior from identity, recognizing that actions can be addressed without defining the individual.

End of Part III Reflection

At this stage, reflection must move beyond external observation and into internal examination. It is necessary to identify the emotional states that most frequently precede financial decisions, as these states provide critical insight into the function of the behavior. Understanding whether spending is linked to stress, boredom, validation, or control allows for more targeted intervention.

Equally important is the examination of identity and perception. Individuals must consider the extent to which their financial behavior is influenced by how they wish to be seen, both by others and by themselves. This includes recognizing instances in which spending is used to reinforce a particular image, rather than to meet a practical need.

The role of entitlement should also be evaluated. This involves assessing how often the concept of deserving is used to justify decisions that may not align with long-term goals. Identifying this pattern allows for a more balanced approach to reward and responsibility.

Finally, reflection must address avoidance. Individuals must consider where they have limited their engagement with financial reality, whether through delayed review, minimized conversations, or selective attention. Recognizing these areas is essential, as avoidance prevents accurate assessment and therefore limits the possibility of change.

The purpose of this reflection is not to assign blame, but to establish understanding. Once the underlying mechanisms of behavior are identified, they can be addressed with intention. Without this understanding, efforts to change behavior will remain inconsistent, as they will not account for the factors that sustain it.

PART IV — THE RELATIONSHIP DAMAGE

Financial infidelity does not remain within individual behavior. While it may originate as a personal pattern, its effects extend outward, influencing the structure and stability of the relationship itself. This expansion is often subtle. It is not always present as overt conflict or immediate breakdown. Instead, it alters the relational environment gradually, introducing inconsistencies that affect trust, communication, and emotional safety.

At its core, a relationship relies on predictability. Not in the sense of rigid routine, but in the alignment between what is said and what is done. When this alignment is disrupted, even in small ways, it introduces uncertainty. Uncertainty, when repeated, leads to observation. Observation, when sustained, leads to doubt. This progression does not require dramatic events. It develops through patterns that may appear insignificant individually but accumulate over time.

What makes this process particularly complex is that it often occurs without direct acknowledgment. The partner affected by the behavior may not immediately confront it. Instead, they register inconsistencies, store observations, and adjust their perception accordingly. This adjustment may not be expressed verbally, but it is reflected in how they engage, respond, and interpret future interactions.

Understanding the relational impact of financial infidelity requires shifting focus from intent to effect. An individual engaging in the behavior may not intend to create instability. However, intent does not negate impact. The relationship responds to what is experienced, not what is meant. Recognizing this distinction is essential, as it reframes the issue from a personal habit to a shared consequence.

Chapter 16 — Perception Without Confrontation: What He Notices

A common assumption in relational dynamics is that the absence of confrontation indicates the absence of awareness. This assumption is often inaccurate. Many individuals do not immediately address discrepancies when they arise. Instead, they observe, collect information, and attempt to make sense of what they are experiencing before initiating discussion.

In the context of financial infidelity, this means that inconsistencies are often recognized long before they are addressed. A charge may not align with a prior explanation. A purchase may appear that was not mentioned. Patterns may emerge that suggest behavior occurring outside of what has been communicated. These observations are not necessarily acted upon immediately, but they are not dismissed.

This process of silent observation alters perception. The partner begins to shift from assumption to analysis, moving away from trust as a default and toward verification as a strategy. This shift is significant, as it changes the foundation upon which the relationship operates. The individual is no longer relying solely on what is said; they are evaluating what is seen.

Importantly, this shift is not always accompanied by overt emotion. It may not present as anger or frustration in the initial stages. Instead, it appears as attentiveness, increased questioning, or a heightened awareness of detail. These changes may be subtle, but they indicate a transition in how the relationship is experienced.

Chapter 17 — The Quiet Erosion of Trust

Trust is often conceptualized as something that is either present or absent. It exists on a continuum. It can strengthen, weaken, or remain stable depending on the consistency of behavior over time. Financial infidelity contributes to a gradual weakening of trust, not through a single event, but through repeated inconsistencies.

This erosion is quiet. It does not always involve confrontation or explicit acknowledgment. Instead, it manifests in small adjustments. Questions become more frequent. Responses are evaluated more closely. Assumptions are replaced with cautious interpretation. The partner begins to rely less on verbal communication and more on observed patterns.

What makes this process particularly impactful is its cumulative nature. Each instance of inconsistency may appear minor in isolation, but together they form a pattern that cannot be easily ignored. Over time, this pattern reshapes the relational dynamic, creating a sense of instability that is difficult to articulate but clearly felt.

An individual engaging in the behavior may not immediately recognize this shift. They may perceive the relationship as unchanged, particularly if no direct conflict has occurred. However, the absence of visible disruption does not indicate the absence of change. Trust does not require a dramatic break to be affected; it can diminish gradually through repeated misalignment.

Chapter 18 — From Patience to Protection

In many relationships, initial responses to inconsistency are characterized by patience. The partner may choose to overlook discrepancies, assuming they are temporary or unintentional. This patience is often grounded in trust, providing space for the behavior to correct itself without immediate confrontation.

However, patience is not indefinite. When inconsistencies persist, the partner begins to reassess their approach. What was initially overlooked becomes noted. What was initially dismissed becomes questioned. This transition marks a shift from patience to protection.

Protection, in this context, does not necessarily involve withdrawal or confrontation. It may manifest as reduced engagement, increased caution, or a reluctance to rely on shared assumptions. The partner begins to adjust their behavior to minimize potential impact, creating a buffer between themselves and the uncertainty introduced by the pattern.

This shift is often experienced as distance. Communication may become more measured. Emotional openness may decrease. The relationship may feel less fluid, less connected, and more structured. These changes are not arbitrary; they are responses to perceived instability.

Chapter 19 — Respect, Consistency, and Relational Stability

Respect within a relationship is closely tied to consistency. When individuals demonstrate alignment between their words and actions, they establish reliability. This reliability fosters confidence, allowing both partners to engage without constant evaluation.

Financial infidelity disrupts this alignment. When behavior is concealed or misrepresented, it introduces inconsistency that affects how the individual is perceived. Over time, this inconsistency may lead to a reevaluation of reliability, influencing not only trust but also respect.

This reevaluation is not necessarily conscious or explicit. It may occur gradually, as patterns are recognized and integrated into the partner's understanding of the relationship. The individual may no longer be seen as inconsistent in isolated moments, but as someone who operates with inconsistency in a particular area.

This perception influences interaction. Communication may become more cautious. Statements may be interpreted with greater scrutiny. The overall dynamic shifts from ease to evaluation, affecting the quality of engagement between partners.

Stability, in this context, is not simply the absence of conflict. It is the presence of predictability and reliability. When these elements are compromised, the relationship may continue to function, but it does so with reduced cohesion and increased tension.

Chapter 20 — The Weight of Imbalance

One of the less visible consequences of financial infidelity is the creation of imbalance within the relationship. This imbalance does not always manifest as overt conflict. Instead, it develops through the uneven distribution of responsibility, awareness, and emotional labor.

When one partner consistently manages the impact of undisclosed or inconsistent behavior, they assume a role that extends beyond shared responsibility. They may find themselves compensating for gaps, addressing issues that arise, or maintaining stability in the face of uncertainty. This change transforms the relationship from a collaborative partnership into a managerial arrangement.

Over time, this shift can create a sense of burden. The partner may feel responsible for maintaining equilibrium, even when they are not the source of the instability. This responsibility, when sustained, can lead to fatigue, disengagement, or resentment.

What makes this dynamic particularly complex is that it may not be openly acknowledged. The relationship may continue without explicit discussion of the imbalance, but the effects are nonetheless present. The partner's experience of the relationship changes, even if the structure remains intact.

Recognizing this imbalance is essential, as it highlights the broader impact of individual behavior. Financial infidelity does not exist in isolation. It influences not only the individual engaging in the behavior, but also the partner who must navigate its consequences.

End of Part IV Reflection

At this stage, reflection must extend beyond personal behavior and consider relational impact. This involves examining how patterns of inconsistency have influenced communication, trust, and emotional engagement within the relationship. It requires identifying changes not only in one's own behavior, but also in the partner's responses.

Attention should be given to shifts in interaction. Have questions become more frequent? Has communication become more cautious or measured? Has there been a noticeable change in emotional availability or engagement? These observations provide insight into how the relationship has adapted to perceived instability.

It is also important to consider the presence of imbalance. Has one partner assumed a greater role in maintaining stability? Are there areas in which responsibility has become uneven? Recognizing these dynamics allows for a more comprehensive understanding of the impact of behavior.

The purpose of this reflection is not to assign blame, but to establish awareness of consequence. Behavior does not exist in isolation; it creates effects that extend beyond the individual. Understanding these effects is essential for meaningful change, as it shifts the focus from personal patterns to shared experience.

PART V — STABILIZE FIRST

Recognition without interruption does not produce change. It produces awareness, and while awareness is necessary, it is not sufficient. Individuals often reach a point where they understand their behavior with clarity yet continue to repeat it. This occurs because understanding does not automatically alter action. Behavior persists until it is disrupted in the moment it occurs.

For this reason, the focus at this stage must shift away from long-term planning and toward immediate stabilization. Many individuals attempt to solve behavioral problems by implementing systems—budgets, tracking tools, and financial plans without first addressing the instability that undermines those systems. The result is predictable. The system fails, not because it is ineffective, but because it is being applied to behavior that has not yet been controlled.

Stabilization requires a different approach. It is not concerned with optimization or efficiency. It is concerned with consistency. The objective is to create a baseline level of control that can support future structure. Without this baseline, any plan, regardless of its quality, will collapse under the weight of unregulated behavior.

This section, therefore, is not about perfecting financial strategy. It is about interrupting the patterns that prevent strategy from working.

Chapter 21 — Control Before Structure

A common misconception in financial behavior is that improved organization will resolve inconsistency. Individuals often believe that if they create a better system, more detailed budgets, more advanced tools, and more structured plans, their behavior will naturally align with it. However, this assumption overlooks a critical factor: systems require adherence.

Without control over decision-making, even the most well-designed system becomes irrelevant. An individual may begin with strong intention, following the plan for a short period of time, only to deviate when faced with emotional triggers or situational pressure. These deviations, when repeated, undermine the system entirely.

This pattern highlights the distinction between intention and execution. Intention reflects what an individual plans to do. Execution reflects what they do under real conditions. The gap between the two is where inconsistency emerges.

Establishing control requires focusing on this gap. It involves developing the ability to pause before acting, to evaluate decisions in real time, and to resist impulses that conflict with stated goals. This is not achieved through planning alone. It is achieved through repeated practice of interruption.

Until this level of control is established, additional structure will not produce meaningful change. It will provide temporary organization, but it will not alter behavior. Control, therefore, must precede structure.

Chapter 22 — The 72-Hour Delay: Creating Decision Space

Impulse thrives immediately. The shorter the time between desire and action, the less opportunity there is for evaluation. For this reason, introducing deliberate delay is one of the most effective methods of interrupting impulsive behavior.

The 72-hour delay functions as a mechanism for creating decision space. By requiring a waiting period before non-essential purchases, the individual disrupts the automatic progression from desire to action. This interruption allows emotional intensity to decrease, providing clarity that is not available in the initial moment.

What is often observed is that the urgency associated with a desired purchase diminishes over time. Items that felt necessary in the moment lose their perceived importance when revisited after a delay. This shift reveals the extent to which initial decisions are influenced by transient emotional states rather than sustained need.

The effectiveness of this approach lies in its simplicity. It does not require complex analysis or extensive planning. It requires only adherence to a clear boundary: if the purchase is not essential, it must wait. This boundary introduces friction into the decision-making process, reducing the likelihood of impulsive action.

Importantly, the delay does not eliminate the possibility of purchase. It ensures that any decision made is intentional rather than reactive. This distinction is central to developing control over behavior.

Chapter 23 — Behavioral Awareness Through the LEDGER Framework

Behavior that is not tracked cannot be accurately evaluated. Individuals often rely on memory or general impressions to assess their actions, leading to incomplete or distorted understanding. To address this limitation, behavior must be documented in a way that captures both action and context.

The LEDGER framework provides a structured method for this documentation. It shifts the focus from financial totals to behavioral patterns, emphasizing the conditions under which decisions are made.

Listing every dollar spent establishes a factual record, eliminating approximation. Identifying the emotional trigger associated with each purchase provides insight into the conditions that drive behavior. Distinguishing between needs and wants clarifies decision-making criteria. Recognizing the gap created by each action highlights consequences beyond the financial. Evaluating patterns over time allows for identification of repetition. Resetting intentionally ensures that adjustments are based on observed behavior rather than assumption.

This process transforms abstract awareness into concrete data. It allows individuals to see their behavior as it occurs, rather than as it is remembered. Over time, patterns become evident, reducing ambiguity and increasing accountability.

The purpose of this framework is not to create restriction, but to establish visibility. Visibility is a prerequisite for change. Without it, behavior remains undefined and therefore difficult to address.

Chapter 24 — Interruption as a Skill, Not a Moment

Many individuals' approach changes as a matter of willpower, expecting that increased motivation will lead to improved outcomes. However, motivation is inconsistent and often influenced by external factors. Relying on it as the primary mechanism for change leads to variability in behavior.

Interruption, by contrast, is a skill that can be developed through practice. It involves recognizing the moment before action and choosing to alter the response. This skill is not dependent on emotional state. It can be applied regardless of motivation.

The critical moment for interruption occurs before the behavior is completed. Once a purchase is made, the opportunity for change has passed. Therefore, attention must be directed toward the earliest stage of the process—the moment of consideration.

In practical terms, this may involve closing an application, stepping away from a device, or redirecting attention to another activity. These actions may appear simple, but their effectiveness lies in their timing. By intervening early, the individual prevents the progression of the behavior.

Developing this skill requires repetition. Each successful interruption reinforces the ability to apply it in future situations. Over time, the behavior becomes less automatic, and the individual gains greater control over their responses.

Chapter 25 — Environmental Design and the Removal of Enablers

Behavior does not occur in isolation from environment. The systems and tools available to an individual influence the ease with which actions can be taken. When environments are structured to minimize friction, behavior becomes more automatic. This is particularly relevant in the context of financial decision-making.

Saved payment methods, one-click purchasing, and multiple access points to funds reduce the effort required to complete a transaction. While these features are designed for convenience, they also facilitate impulsive behavior. The absence of friction eliminates the natural pause that might otherwise occur before a decision is finalized.

To counteract this effect, the environment must be intentionally modified. Removing saved payment information, limiting access to credit-based spending, and consolidating accounts introduces friction into the process. This friction is not a limitation; it is a control mechanism.

By increasing the effort required to complete a purchase, the individual creates an opportunity for evaluation. The additional steps provide time for reconsideration, reducing the likelihood of impulsive action.

Environmental design, therefore, becomes an extension of behavioral control. It supports the development of consistent patterns by aligning external conditions with internal goals.

End of Part V Reflection

Reflection at this stage must focus on the practical application of control. It is necessary to identify areas in which behavior remains inconsistent, particularly in moments of decision-making. This involves examining situations in which impulses override intention and determining what conditions contributed to that outcome.

The effectiveness of delay should also be considered. Individuals must assess whether introducing time between desire and action has altered their decision-making process. Identifying purchases that would have been avoided through delay provides evidence of their impact.

Behavioral tracking must be evaluated for accuracy and consistency. Partial or inconsistent documentation limits the usefulness of the data collected. Ensuring that all relevant actions are recorded allows for a more complete understanding of patterns.

Environmental factors should be reviewed as well. Identifying systems that facilitate impulsive behavior allows for targeted modification. Removing or altering these systems supports the development of control.

The purpose of this reflection is to transition from awareness to action. Behavior change is not achieved through understanding alone. It requires consistent application of strategies that interrupt existing patterns and support the development of new ones.

PART VI — THE CONVERSATION

Behavior can be modified privately, but relational damage cannot be repaired in isolation. At some point, internal awareness must translate into external communication. This transition is often the most difficult stage, not because individuals lack understanding, but because communication introduces vulnerability. It requires being seen clearly, without the protection of explanation, minimization, or delay.

Many individuals attempt to resolve financial infidelity by correcting behavior without addressing its history. They reduce spending, increase awareness, and implement control strategies, believing that visible improvement will eliminate the need for conversation. However, this approach overlooks a critical reality: patterns that have already been observed do not disappear simply because behavior changes. The partner has already experienced inconsistency. That experience deserves recognition.

The purpose of this section is not to script a perfect conversation, but to establish principles for communication that reflect accountability, clarity, and consistency. Communication, in this context, is not about persuasion. It is about alignment between what is said and what is done moving forward.

Chapter 26 — The Conversation Is Not Optional

Avoidance is often rationalized as timing. Individuals may delay conversations under the assumption that it is better to address the issue once they have fully corrected their behavior. While this reasoning may appear logical, it is fundamentally flawed. Delaying communication does not resolve the underlying issue; it extends the period during which the partner remains uninformed.

When patterns have existed, they leave traces. These traces may take the form of observed inconsistencies, unanswered questions, or unresolved concerns. Even if they have not been expressed directly, they influence perception. Attempting to bypass the conversation ignores this reality.

The necessity of communication lies in its function. It provides context, establishes clarity, and creates an opportunity for alignment. Without it, the partner is left to interpret behavior independently, often filling gaps with assumptions. These assumptions, once formed, can be difficult to correct.

Engaging in the conversation requires accepting that discomfort is unavoidable. It is not an indication that something is wrong; it is a natural response to confronting a pattern that has been previously concealed. The objective is not to eliminate discomfort, but to engage with it constructively.

Chapter 27 — Questions as Indicators of Trust Assessment

When a partner begins to ask questions about financial behavior, the focus is often placed on the content of those questions. However, the more significant element is the context in which they are asked. Questions, in this scenario, function as indicators of trust assessment. They reflect an effort to reconcile observed behavior with communicated information.

The way these questions are answered plays a critical role in shaping perception. Responses that are vague, defensive, or overly complex introduce additional uncertainty. They suggest that information is being managed rather than shared.

In contrast, direct and concise responses reduce ambiguity. They provide clear information without unnecessary elaboration. This clarity supports the rebuilding of trust by demonstrating consistency between communication and behavior.

It is important to recognize that the partner is not only evaluating the answer itself, but the way it is delivered. Tone, timing, and clarity all contribute to the overall impression. Communication, therefore, must be approached with intentionality, ensuring that responses align with the objective of transparency.

Chapter 28 — The Distinction Between Explanation and Ownership

One of the most common barriers to effective communication is the tendency to prioritize explanation over ownership. Explanation involves providing context, reasoning, and background information to clarify behavior. While context can be valuable, it becomes problematic when it replaces accountability.

Ownership, by contrast, is characterized by direct acknowledgment of behavior without deflection. It does not attempt to reduce the significance of the action or shift focus to contributing factors. Instead, it establishes a clear understanding of what occurred and accepts responsibility for it.

The distinction between these two approaches is subtle but significant. Explanation often extends the conversation, introducing additional variables that may obscure the central issue. Ownership simplifies the conversation, focusing on the behavior itself and the commitment to change.

This does not mean that context should never be provided. Rather, it should follow ownership, not replace it. Establishing accountability first creates a foundation upon which context can be understood without diminishing responsibility.

Chapter 29 — Responding to Frustration Without Escalation

Frustration is a natural response to perceived inconsistency. When a partner expresses frustration, the instinctive reaction may be to defend, justify, or counter the expression. However, these responses often escalate the situation, shifting the focus from resolution to conflict.

Effective response requires a different approach. It involves acknowledging the frustration without attempting to negate it. This acknowledgment does not imply agreement with every aspect of the expression; it demonstrates recognition of its validity within the partner's experience.

By validating the emotional response, the individual creates space for constructive dialogue. This approach reduces defensiveness and allows the conversation to remain focused on resolution rather than escalation.

It is also important to recognize that frustration may persist even after behavior has begun to change. This persistence is not an indication that progress is ineffective; it reflects the time required for perception to adjust. Patience, in this context, is not passive. It is an active component of rebuilding trust.

Chapter 30 — Rebuilding Trust Through Consistent Behavior

Trust, once disrupted, cannot be restored through verbal assurance alone. It is rebuilt through consistent alignment between communication and behavior over time. This process is incremental, requiring repeated demonstration of reliability in situations that previously involved inconsistency.

Consistency serves as evidence. Each instance in which behavior aligns with communicated expectations reinforces the perception of reliability. Over time, these instances accumulate, gradually shifting the partner's assessment from uncertainty to confidence.

It is important to understand that this process does not follow a fixed timeline. The rate at which trust is rebuilt depends on the consistency of behavior and the extent of the previous pattern. Attempting to accelerate the process through reassurance or pressure is often counterproductive, as it places emphasis on outcome rather than behavior.

Rebuilding trust also involves initiative-taking communication. This includes sharing information without prompting, addressing potential concerns before they arise, and maintaining transparency even in situations that may feel uncomfortable. These actions demonstrate a commitment to change that extends beyond reactive response.

Trust is not rebuilt in a single moment. It is reconstructed through a series of consistent actions that, over time, establish a new pattern. This pattern becomes the basis for renewed confidence in the relationship.

End of Part VI Reflection

Reflection at this stage must focus on communication patterns and their alignment with behavioral change. It is necessary to evaluate not only what has been said, but how it has been communicated. This includes assessing the clarity, tone, and timing of responses to questions or concerns.

Individuals must also consider the balance between explanation and ownership. Determining whether accountability has been clearly established, or whether it has been obscured by context, provides insight into the effectiveness of communication.

The response to frustration should be examined as well. Identifying whether reactions have contributed to escalation or resolution allows for adjustment in future interactions. This includes recognizing instances in which defensiveness may have limited the potential for constructive dialogue.

Finally, reflection must address consistency. Evaluating whether behavior has aligned with communicated intentions over time provides a measure of progress. Consistency is the primary mechanism through which trust is rebuilt, and its presence or absence is central to the outcome of the process.

The purpose of this reflection is to ensure that communication supports, rather than undermines, behavioral change. Without alignment between the two, progress remains incomplete.

The Non-Returnable Receipt

Before you write anything down, pause.

Not for a second. Not casually.
Pause long enough to feel what you've been avoiding.

This section is not about performance. It is not about writing what sounds good, what feels acceptable, or what you think should be true. This is about accuracy.

Because the truth—when it is finally acknowledged without adjustment—is often uncomfortable. Not because it is harsh, but because it is clear. And clarity removes your ability to pretend.

You already know where you've been dishonest.
You already know what you've been avoiding.
You already know what you've minimized.

This is where you stop negotiating with yourself.

You are not filling out a worksheet.
You are documenting reality.

And once it is written honestly…
you don't get to say you didn't know anymore.

MY FINANCIAL TRUTH

Fill this out with full honesty.

No soft language. No rounding. No “kind of.”

Write it exactly as it is.

Financial Reality Overview

Total current debt (be exact, not estimated):

How long has this debt been building (months/years)?

What have you told yourself about this number to avoid dealing with it?

Hidden Behavior Inventory

Hidden purchases (be specific—what, when, and why you didn't say anything):

____

____

____

____

Accounts, cards, or apps he does not know about (include everything):

____

____

____

Subscriptions you ignored, forgot, or avoided canceling:

____

____

____

Money you redirected, repurposed, or misrepresented:

Pattern Recognition (This Is Where It Gets Real)

What patterns are now obvious that you can no longer deny?
(Examples: emotional spending, hiding purchases, avoidance, delayed truth)

What situations trigger your worst financial decisions?

What emotions show up right before you spend irresponsibly?

____

____

____

Accountability Without Excuses

What have these behaviors already cost you?
(Be specific: trust, peace, stability, confidence)

____

____

____

If nothing changes, what will this cost you next?

____

____

____

Commitment

What are you committing to changing starting today—specifically and measurably?

What will you stop doing immediately (no gradual reduction)?

What will you start doing consistently (even when you don't feel like it)?

30-DAY FINANCIAL INTEGRITY RESET (EXPANDED SYSTEM)

You are not rebuilding this with feelings.
You are rebuilding this with structure, repetition, and discipline.

Each week builds on the previous one.
Do not skip ahead. Do not modify the order.

WEEK 1 — AWARENESS (YOU FACE EVERYTHING)

Objective: Remove avoidance completely.

You are not fixing anything this week.
You are seeing everything.

[ ] Write down every single purchase (no exceptions)
[ ] Check all bank accounts daily (not "when you feel like it")
[ ] Review receipts instead of throwing them away
[ ] Track exact amounts (no rounding, no estimating)
[ ] Look at your total balances—even if it makes you uncomfortable

Additional Required Action:

What did you feel when you saw your numbers clearly?

What surprised you the most?

WEEK 2 — HONESTY (YOU STOP HIDING)

Objective: Eliminate secrecy.

[ ] No hidden purchases—everything is visible

[ ] No delayed truth ("I'll mention it later" is no longer allowed)

[ ] Answer financial questions directly and clearly

[ ] Admit past behaviors without minimizing

[ ] Stop reframing your behavior to make it sound smaller

Additional Required Action:

Where did you feel tempted to hide something this week?

What did you do instead?

WEEK 3 — DISCIPLINE (YOU CONTROL YOURSELF)

Objective: Interrupt impulsive behavior.

[ ] No impulse spending

[ ] 72-hour pause before all non-essential purchases

[ ] Follow a strict spending boundary (define it clearly)

[ ] Remove saved cards and payment shortcuts

[ ] Avoid known emotional spending triggers

Additional Required Action:

What purchase did you avoid that you normally would have made?

What did you learn about your impulses?

WEEK 4 — ALIGNMENT (YOU MOVE DIFFERENTLY)

Objective: Become consistent—not temporary.

[ ] Have a direct financial conversation without defensiveness

[ ] Share actual numbers (not edited versions)

[ ] Create a simple, realistic plan together

[ ] Establish clear expectations around spending

[ ] Commit to full transparency moving forward

Additional Required Action:

What felt different about your behavior this week?

____

Where are you still struggling?

____

____

RELATIONSHIP REBUILD CHECKLIST

If you want to rebuild what this affected, understand this clearly:

Apologies are not repair.
Consistency is.

Foundational Requirements

[ ] Full financial transparency (no hidden areas)

[ ] No defensiveness when asked questions

[ ] Willingness to show accounts without hesitation

[ ] Consistent honesty—not selective honesty

[ ] Regular financial conversations (not only when problems arise)

Behavioral Alignment

[ ] You communicate before spending—not after

[ ] You no longer "manage the narrative"

[ ] Your actions match your words consistently

[ ] You stop minimizing your behavior when addressed

Relational Stability

[ ] You respect boundaries that are set

[ ] You contribute to emotional safety—not confusion

[ ] You allow time for trust to rebuild without rushing it

[ ] You accept that consistency must be proven—not assumed

ESSENCE TRUTH

You just didn't make financial mistakes.
You created patterns that required concealment.

It was never about the money.
It was about the decisions you didn't want to explain.

You don't rebuild trust by saying "I've changed."
You rebuild trust by becoming predictable in your behavior.

Financial security is not created by income alone.
It is created by discipline, honesty, and consistency.

You cannot keep labeling something as "small"
when its impact keeps showing up in significant ways.

TO THE MAN WHO STAYED ANYWAY

You paid attention when things didn't add up.
You noticed what wasn't said as much as what was.

You carried questions you didn't always ask.
You gave space when you could have pushed.

You stayed present in a situation that required patience,
even when clarity would have been easier.

This book may not center your voice,
but it acknowledges your experience.

And to the woman reading this:

Do not confuse his patience with permission.
Do not use his consistency as an excuse to remain inconsistent.

KEEP DOING THE WORK

This is not a one-time realization.
It is a behavioral shift that must be practiced repeatedly.

You are not trying to become perfect.
You are becoming consistent.

You are not trying to impress anyone.
You are becoming accountable.

You are not just changing how you spend.
You are changing how you decide.

And that shift will show up in everything—
your money, your communication, your confidence, and your relationships.

90-DAY CONTINUATION TRACKER (NEW SECTION)

Month 1: ______________________________

Month 2: ______________________________

Month 3: ______________________________

Biggest improvement so far:

____

Biggest challenge still exists:

____

One behavior that is no longer part of your life:

____

____

www.ingramcontent.com/pod-product-compliance
Lightning Source LLC
LaVergne TN
LVHW010626100826
845148LV00014B/3127

* 9 7 9 8 9 0 0 8 3 5 0 2 0 *